ANIMALS EXPOSED!

The Truth About
Animal Communication

Created and produced by Firecrest Books Ltd
in association with the
John Francis Studio/Bernard Thornton Artists

Published by Tangerine Press,
an imprint of Scholastic Inc;
557 Broadway, New York, NY 10012

ISBN 0-439-54329-0

Printed and bound in Thailand
First Printing June 2003

The Truth About Animal Communication

Bernard Stonehouse
and Esther Bertram

Illustrated by
John Francis

Tangerine Press and associated logo
and design are trademarks of Scholastic Inc.

FOR SIÂN

Art and Editorial Direction by
Peter Sackett

Edited by
Norman Barrett

Designed by
Paul Richards, Designers & Partners

Color separation by
**SC (Sang Choy) International Pte Ltd
Singapore**

Printed and bound by
Sirivatana Interprint Public Co., Thailand

Contents

Exchanging Information   6

Sound the Alarm   8

This is My Space   10

Personal Warning   12

Danger Warnings   14

Living in Harmony   16

Working Together   18

Poisonous Warnings   20

Love at First Sight   22

Watch out, I'm Angry   24

Showing Who's Boss   26

Among Friends   28

Care and Attention   30

Animal Courtship   32

Holding the Attraction   34

Fighting Rivals   36

Show the Way   38

Friend or Foe?   40

Learn by Play   42

Watch my Face   44

Mutual Cooperation   46

Index   48

Exchanging Information

Do animals talk to each other? How do they tell each other about the world? Humans are the only animals with words to say what we mean. So we talk and write words to each other. Only a few animals have anything like words: They tell each other things in vocal ways. Lions roar, birds twitter and sing, frogs croak, crickets chirp. These are all animals telling other animals about themselves. They usually talk to their own kind, but their messages can come across to other species, too. They have many other ways of communicating. Chimpanzees grin, wolves show their teeth, horses set their ears back and curl up their lips, cats rub up against us and each other. These are also messages, conveyed not by sounds, but by behavior – something that one animal does and another recognizes. Other animals release scents, telling others where to find them or that others need to stay away. These messages are very important, but how they are sent is very simple communication.

We can tune into many of the messages that pass between animals, but we must be careful not to interpret them in human terms. We smile when we are content; does the chimpanzee's grin show that it is content? We shout, or roar, if we are angry; is a roaring lion angry? We sing when we are happy; is a singing bird happy, too? Many myths surround animal communication, but the truth may be different and far more interesting. Read on about how animals communicate, and what they tell each other through sounds, scents, and displays.

To us, this rooster may be saying "Good morning." To other roosters, his message is, "This is my territory and these are my hens. Stay away!"

When the sentry barks his warning, he and the other prairie dogs scurry for safety down the nearest tunnel.

Barking a warning
Meerkats (a kind of mongoose) live on the plains of southern Africa, in family groups of 20 to 30 adults. Like prairie dogs, they live in burrows. Watchers sit upright on

Sound the Alarm

Many people think that prairie dogs are members of the dog family. After all, they are called dogs and they bark, so surely they must be dogs. But, no – prairie dogs are rodents, like rats and squirrels. People call them dogs because they bark like watchdogs when alarmed. About the size of rabbits, they live on the grasslands of North America, feeding on grasses and herbs. Several hundreds of them live together in burrows called towns.

When feeding, some act as sentries, staying on the lookout for hawks, foxes, and other predators. If a sentry sees something dangerous, it barks loudly, then heads for the safety of the tunnels. When one barks, the others all bark and disappear.

It is usually the males that keep watch, while the females are feeding, or busy below ground tending their babies. They are all alert all the time, but standing guard takes energy and is not very productive. So just a few keep watch, while the rest go about their business. All they need to do to be safe is respond quickly to danger signals – the watcher's bark.

Cackling calls

On the African plains you often find mixed herds of zebras and ostriches. Zebras feed like horses, grazing in the long grass with their heads down. Standing taller, ostriches are usually first to see danger. Zebras have learned to respond to their cackling calls.

Thumping and bobbing

Wild rabbits, brindled or dark brown, have white stubby tails that hardly show when they are resting or sitting up to watch. A rabbit sensing danger thumps the ground with its hind feet, then runs for cover. The thumping and the bobbing white tail warn the rest that it is time to hide.

This is My Space

Opposite page: A pouch inside the throat magnifies the sound, so the treetop call of the howler monkey can be heard for miles.

Animals that move in groups like to keep space around them so they can feed and go about their business in peace. Do they fight for their space? Not necessarily. If they make enough noise, they can scare others into staying away.

Howler monkeys feed on fruit, fresh shoots, leaves, and insects up in the tops of high forest trees. They tell others of their kind where they are by emitting long, howling calls. Usually one male starts the call from high in a tree, yelling with wide-open mouth. Others of the troop join in, until 20 or 30 are calling loudly together. The sound travels far on the still air. When other troops several miles away hear them, they start their own chorus, and soon the forest is ringing with howler monkey calls. That way each troop gets to know where the other monkeys are feeding, and all can stay out of each other's way.

Buzzing

Tiny bees can drive off much larger animals with their buzzing and painful stings. This young fox has stuck its nose into a wild bees' nest, and it is learning a painful lesson. If the stings don't kill him, he'll remember that buzzing means pain. Next time he hears bees, he'll stay away from them.

Baying at the moon?

Groups of wolves tell each other where they are by baying, or howling, in chorus. Do they bay at the moon? Not especially. They call during the day, too, but you hear them most often on moonlit nights, when the rest of the forest is silent and they are out hunting.

Roaring

Lions cough, grunt, and growl quietly to others within their pride or family group. They use their loud roar to tell other groups that they are near. This big male lion is roaring to signal that his group has moved into the area, and others better stay away.

Wafting scent

Troops of Madagascan lemurs, meeting each other in forest clearings, sometimes stalk up and down with striped tails waving in the air like banners. The tails carry each group's scent. Meeting on the boundary of their territories, the groups are sending the message, "You're different from us. Don't come any closer."

Personal Warning

Singing a warning

Do birds sing when they are happy? We don't know, but we do know that singing can be a warning message to other birds of the same species. On an early spring evening, this blackbird is singing from a treetop. Other male blackbirds will take it as a warning to stay away.

Birds of a feather flock together? Yes, but not always. Flocks of wild geese fly long distances between breeding and wintering grounds, and they feed together in groups like big families. But when they are nesting and rearing their young, pairs of geese want to be alone, and they become quite fierce if others come near them. This gander (male goose) is guarding a nest in the long grass near where his mate is incubating seven blue-white eggs. She sits very quietly while he walks up and down, drawing attention to himself and away from the nest. If other geese or possible predators come by, he honks noisily and hisses at them. If they come too close, he rushes at them with bill open and wings spread. He can peck hard and beat off predators such as owls and arctic foxes with those strong wings. Meanwhile, his mate sits quietly, keeping the eggs warm until they hatch into goslings.

Right: This gander's nest is nearby. His ruffled feathers, wide eyes, gaping bill, and honking are warnings: "Move away or I'll come after you."

Crowing a warning

This rooster lives on a farm, but he's doing just what his wild ancestors did long ago. He and his hens are scratching and pecking for insects, seeds, and fresh green food. From time to time he crows loudly. Other roosters hear and stay away. If they come too close, he'll attack and chase them off.

Leaving a scent

Rabbits have a great sense of smell, and they use scents as messages for each other. This male rabbit, rubbing his chin on a stone, leaves an oily scent that lasts for several days. Other rabbits smelling it will know that there is a mature male rabbit nearby. Females may want to find him, but other males will keep their distance.

Locking horns

During the breeding season, male Thomson's gazelles take up territories of a few dozen square yards, and wait for groups of females to come by. Males meeting at the territory boundaries often lower their heads, lock horns, and push against each other. Lowering the head is a challenge, meaning, "Let's see which of us can push harder."

Danger Warnings

Scary "eyes"

Lantern bugs live among the shrubs of South American woodlands. With its greeny-brown wing cases and long, mottled proboscis, or nose, one sitting at rest

could easily be mistaken for a rolled-up leaf. But touch it, even lightly, and those two wings spring open, with golden-yellow spots that look a lot like eyes. That is usually enough to scare a predatory bird or small mammal that might be in search of a meal.

It's a common belief that snakes strike without warning. But is this true? Not really. Snakes are usually silent, staying out of the way of other animals. They have no vocal cords, so they cannot roar, croak, sing, squeak, or bark.

However, most snakes hiss when disturbed, tiny ones quietly, bigger ones more loudly. If you step on one, it may try to bite you, but it will usually hiss first.

Rattlesnakes always give a warning. Different species live throughout North America. Dark reddish-brown or black, they match their backgrounds well, and are hard to see. Their rattle is a group of up to a dozen hollow, dried-skin shells on the end of the tail. When the snake is alarmed, it shakes its tail, making a sound like dry bones in a box. Standing within a few feet, you are likely to hear the rattle before you see the snake. So the rattlesnake shakes its rattle when large animals are nearby, warning them to walk carefully. This gives the snake a chance to get to safety.

Opposite page: The rattlesnake is alarmed and shaking its rattle, a warning to cattle and other large animals not to step on it.

Smelly warning

The North American skunk defends itself from predators by shooting a foul-smelling liquid from glands under its tail – enough to keep any animal away that threatens to attack it. A predator that has been sprayed by one skunk won't want to mess with another one. The eye-catching black and white fur is a visual reminder to stay away.

Warning signals

Here is a wildcat in a bad mood. Something, perhaps another cat, has scared it, so it is signaling a warning. Ears back, whiskers flat to the face, eyes staring, mouth open, hissing, and spitting – the message is clear: "Stay away or I'll bite."

Spitting a warning

Llamas are South American mammals related to African and Asian camels. Standing about 4 ft. (1.2 m) tall, they are farmed for their fine wool, and are normally calm and easy to handle. However, watch out for a frightened or angry llama. It may raise its ears, stare, and spit part of its last meal.

Living in Harmony

Opposite page: Male flamingos band together and race across the lake shallows, attracting the females that will become their mates.

Finding food

Some kinds of birds, such as these rooks, spend their time in big flocks. You seldom see one on its own. Flocking birds benefit where food is sparse. Here a few have found a patch of grass with plenty of insects. The others saw them feeding, and have flown down to join in.

Is safety found in numbers? When thousands of birds nest together in colonies, they far outnumber the local predators, so only the ones around the edges are likely to be killed. Flamingos breed in colonies of tens or hundreds of thousands on shallow lakes and lagoons from South America to central Asia. A hundred thousand flamingos, splendid in pink and white plumage, make a remarkable sight, especially during courtship. They usually breed in spring.

To ensure that they all breed around the same time, males band together in courtship displays.

Kissing and smelling

Prairie dogs (see also pages 8–9) spend much of their lives in burrows. How do family members find each other in the dark? Mainly by smell: They come close to each other and seem to kiss, recognizing each other's scent.

The males race together across the shallow water with heads weaving and bills pointing to the sky. The few that start become a signal for others to join in, until thousands are racing in colorful swarms back and forth across the lake.

Follow the leader

Gnus, or wildebeest, live in huge herds on the African plains. Like sheep, they follow each other. Any gnu that starts walking, firmly signals, "I know the way," and soon has others trotting behind. On long seasonal migrations, old, experienced bulls become the herd leaders.

Getting to know you

Gorillas live in family bands that roam through the African rainforests. Within small groups, individuals spend months and years in each other's company, and they get to know one another well. They communicate in grunts and squeals, but they also learn by watching others' facial expressions and body movements. Here a small group has spent the day feeding and is resting in the late afternoon sun. The young one sees the grown-ups relaxing, so he sits quietly alongside – at least for the moment.

Left: Gentoo penguins find safety by staying together, following each other down to the sea, and watching for leopard seals, their main predator.

Attack in numbers

Orcas, also called killer whales, are fierce hunters of seals and sea lions. Though a seal might get away from a single orca, it has less chance of outswimming a dozen. In polar waters, orcas look for seals sleeping on small ice floes. One tips the floe, and the others grab the seal as it rolls off.

Working Together

Do penguins push each other into the water to see if seals are around? It's a good story, but not really true.

Penguins live in groups and follow each other both at sea and on land. These gentoo penguins, about 100 of them, have left the breeding colony and headed for the sea to go fishing. A particularly hungry penguin started the procession, and the others followed.

But leopard seals, their main predators, may lie in wait for them just beyond the surf, so the penguins have to be sure there are none around. They parade up and down along the shore, peering out at the sea. If one penguin sees a black head bobbing in the water, that could be a seal. The penguin leads the way back up the beach, the others follow, and all forget about swimming for an hour or two.

Then they parade again. If no black heads appear this time, the first few dive into the water, the others follow, and all swim to the feeding grounds. With no words exchanged, a hundred penguins have started their journey safely.

Alerting the sleepers
Large lizards called marine iguanas live on the shores of the Galapagos Islands in the Pacific Ocean. After feeding in the sea, they haul themselves out to rest in huddles on the rocks, some sleeping, others keeping an eye open for danger. If a hawk appears, the watchers stand upright, alerting the sleepers.

Following the trail
Bred especially for hunting, these foxhounds work like wild dogs. All sniff the ground until one smells a fresh fox trail. It calls, then follows the trail head-down. The others might not have caught the scent, but they follow the leader in full cry.

Mobbing
Finches, chickadees, and other small songbirds cannot ignore an owl. If one sees an owl sleeping quietly in a tree, it flies around calling noisily and darting with claws spread. Others join in, mobbing continually until the owl flies off. It pays for them to gang up on a sleeping owl.

Poisonous Warnings

Don't step on me
Coral snakes are a group of brightly banded snakes from North and South America, South Africa, and the Far East. Their vivid colors and poisonous fangs are the common threads for the different species. The colors warn larger animals not to step on them. They won't do any harm unless they are disturbed. Other snakes mimic the colors of the coral snake.

Left: The ladybug's brightly colored casing splits down the back to expose strong, transparent wings. Ladybugs fly in search of aphids, their main food source.

If you are small, it would be safest to hide, or is that always true? Dozens of kinds of ladybugs tell us no. All are small, but with the brightest of wing cases – red with black spots; black with red spots; yellow, brown, or black with contrasting spots or stripes. We see ladybugs sitting on leaves or flying on wings that fold away under the colored casing. Gardeners love them. Both adults and larvae feed on aphids and other small, soft-bodied pests.

Why are ladybugs brightly colored when other animals find it safer to hide? It's because their main defense is a strong smell, and they have a taste that birds and other predators find unpleasant. The coloring reminds predators that have found one ladybug distasteful – stay away from all other small beetles with bright colors and spots, because they may taste nasty, too.

Orange for danger
Small, brightly colored poison dart frogs live in trees high in the damp rainforests of South America. Again, the bright colors indicate danger. These frogs contain a nerve crippling poison, deadly to animals that try to eat them. Native hunters use the poison to tip arrows.

Colorful reminder
We call this a scorpionfish, but the same name is given to more than 300 different kinds of fish, mostly with brilliant colors. Nearly all have spines that sting like land scorpions, and they can hurt anything they touch. The stings and poison are protective. The colors remind predators that these are dangerous fish that are best left alone.

Surprise warning
Small, fire-bellied toads seem harmless and dull at first sight – gray, brown-speckled, or black on top, with only a hint of color under the chin. When alarmed, they fall backward to expose vivid colors underneath – red, orange, or yellow, according to species. This signals a distasteful and even poisonous skin.

Love at First Sight

Opposite page: This male anole lizard develops a fold of colored skin on his throat – an attraction to females and a warning to other males.

Animals cannot lie; only humans can. Is that so? Well, a lot of animals stretch the truth – for example, about their size. Often it pays a small animal to look as big as it can, or to exaggerate its size to show off before rivals.

This male anole lizard of South American forests lives quietly and inconspicuously for much of the year, climbing trunks and crawling along branches in search of insects, snails, and other small items of food. Pale yellowish-brown, with darker bands and spots, it is camouflaged well: Predatory birds have to look hard to find it. During the breeding season, when rival males meet, anoles make themselves look as big as possible. Each turns sideways, raises itself on all four legs, lifts its tail, and expands the pale skin under its throat into a vivid orange patch. After a few moments of display, one or the other – usually the smaller – backs off and disappears. The same display attracts females for mating.

Changing shape
Porcupine fish from warm tropical seas look like any other slender, slippery fish as they swim about the reefs and sea floor, nibbling for food. When threatened or alarmed, they change shape, rounding themselves into a solid, spine-covered ball that no predator would want to tackle.

Expanding head
Widespread throughout Africa, India, and southern and southeast Asia, cobras are snakes with a crest or hood on either side of the neck. Hardly showing in a resting cobra, the hood expands when the animal becomes excited, making the snake more visible and perhaps more fearsome to its enemies.

Inflatable nose
Hooded seals live on the floating ice of the Arctic Ocean, well out to sea on either side of Greenland. Gathering for mating in early spring, males develop a huge inflatable hood, or bladder, on their nose and foreheads. This makes them look bigger during courtship and probably makes them sound bigger when they roar at each other.

Raising feathers
Swans have little to fear from the smaller birds that share their nesting grounds. But during the breeding season, mated pairs defend their nests and feeding areas from rival swans. When rivals meet at their territory boundaries, each swan turns sideways, raising its feathers and wings, and making itself look as big and formidable as possible. Rivals seldom fight. After displaying, each heads for home.

Baboons living closely in troops get to know each other's moods and expressions. This male's face shows anger and threat – clear warnings for others to stay away.

Watch Out, I'm Angry

Range of expressions

Desert cats of Africa and southwest Asia, caracals are bigger and more slender than most domestic cats, though equally capable of sharing their lives with humans. Like wildcats, they have a range of facial expressions. These erect, tufted ears and open mouth signal interest and a possible attack.

Do animals show emotions? Do they get angry like we do? We don't really know what animals feel about themselves. We can only watch to see what they do and judge their feelings from their actions. Mammals in general, and monkeys and apes in particular, often show what looks like frustration or anger in circumstances that would cause us stress.

Here is a male baboon in a very bad mood. Perhaps he has been robbed of food or frightened by a bigger rival. He has pulled back his head, opened his mouth wide, tightened his lips to show his rows of sharp teeth, and is roaring loudly.

These are signals that other baboons would recognize and know how to handle. He is excited and ready for a fight. The message is, "Keep away or get bitten," a warning to neighbors to stay out of reach until he has calmed down. Other animals signal dangerous moods in similar ways.

About to charge

African elephants weigh 5 to 6 tons, and have few natural enemies. Normally peaceable, they are likely to become aggressive when guarding their young. However, they give plenty of warning. Ears pulled forward, intensive staring, often a restless stamping with both feet, are an elephant's signals that it may charge. When an elephant charges, other animals should stay out of its way.

Neighborly warning

Skinks are lively lizards that live in warm climates and feed on insects and other small animals. Each keeps a space around itself, so it can see others coming. If a neighbor approaches, this blue-tongued skink sticks out its bright blue tongue, a warning to others that its next move may be to attack.

Bored or angry?

If a hippopotamus (right) opens its mouth and yawns toward you, is it bored with your company? If it does it toward another hippo, it is probably angry. The yawn shows its large teeth and its intention of lumbering forward and biting them – unless it forgets and goes to sleep first.

Showing Who's Boss

Stay cool
The sea lion's whiskers are used mainly in underwater hunting. On the breeding grounds, when dominant bulls get excited and threaten to fight each other, cows calm them down by nuzzling their whiskers. The message: "You're the boss; why fight?"

Signaling submission
Like other young animals that live in groups with adults, zebra colts have to find their position in society. A young zebra normally carries its head up and ears forward. If bullied by an elder, it signals submission by lowering its head and setting its ears back.

Ears are for hearing, but they have other uses, too. Bat-eared foxes live in desert scrublands of central and eastern Africa. The big ears help with hearing: When these foxes are hunting for insects and other small animals, the ears are erect and twitching, alert for the slightest sounds. They are also radiators, helping the fox to keep cool on hot dry days. No less important, they are signals in the animals' social life. Like other foxes, dogs, and wolves, bat-eared foxes live in small family groups, in which some, usually the older ones, dominate or boss the others. They may fight over which is the boss, but fighting with sharp teeth can cause a lot of damage. Displaying makes better sense. Here the fox on the right is boss, signaled by his stance, erect tail, and the forward position of his ears. The smaller, younger animal, lies down with tail tucked under and ears back, signaling submission.

Bringing gifts
As with kittiwakes (see above) and many other kinds of birds, a cormorant returning to its nest must immediately make peace with its partner, who may otherwise mistake it for a stranger and attack. Often the one flying in brings a present of nesting material – possibly seaweed or grass picked up at the last moment – and lays it on the edge of the nest. In the time it takes for the sitting bird to pick up the material and add it to the nest, the two come to recognize and accept each other.

No room for fighting
Kittiwakes – a kind of gull – court, incubate, and raise their chicks on very narrow cliff ledges. When one of a pair returns to the nest, it needs to show submission to its partner to avoid being attacked. Other gulls often display a noisy, energetic exchange of calls and bows. Kittiwakes on their ledges exchange signals very gently to avoid knocking eggs or chicks out of the nest.

The bat-eared fox on the right is leader of the group. The smaller one is showing submission and complete acceptance of his leadership.

Among Friends

Animals are *wild*. Can they become close friends as well? Even among herd animals, the adults try to keep space around them. Others coming close may hurt or kill them, steal their food, or pass diseases or parasites to them.

Keeping space works until the time comes for breeding. Then individuals must stop signaling, "Keep your distance," and signal instead, "Come closer and stay by me." That way they find a partner, form a pair, and share territory, den, and family. It is a big change in behavior, often depending on changes in hormones – the chemical messengers from the brain that kick-start breeding behavior.

Mourning doves, which live in big flocks of several dozen, stay apart from each other until the breeding season, when they come closer together. Then each male finds a nest site and attracts a female to it. Once a pair has accepted each other, they caress and preen each other constantly, getting used to having each other around, and strengthening the bond between them.

Mutual preening
Both birds and mammals gain pleasure from preening their own feathers or fur, almost as much as they enjoy preening others of their kind, especially within the same family group. It is useful, too. Chimpanzees remove parasites, twigs, and leaves from each other's fur, and comb it with their fingers.

Tail-wagging
Domestic dogs, just like wild ones, are usually suspicious on meeting, walking on tiptoe with fur on the neck and back raised, and sniffing each other's scent glands (the ones beneath the tail) to see if they belong to a familiar group. That done, a lick, and a wagging tail show that they accept each other as friends.

Left: Mourning doves, nesting in the safety of a prickly pear cactus, preen each other's feathers. This helps keep them clean, and it also strengthens the partnership.

Wallowing together
During the breeding season, male elephant seals stay away from each other, maintaining the territories in which the females raise their young, and keeping other males out by roaring and fighting. Once breeding is over, the males lie close together in muddy wallows, keeping each other warm while they molt their fur and outer skin.

Renewing partnerships
Albatrosses breed in large colonies, usually on the same nest and with the same mate each year. Each partner, in turn, incubates and broods the

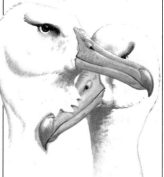

chick, while the other flies hundreds of miles over the ocean in search of food. On the wanderer's return, mutual preening helps them renew their partnership.

Animal Courtship

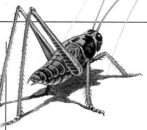

Left: The red throat pouch of a male frigatebird inflates – a signal to females that he is ready for courtship and mating.

We tend to think that mating in nature just happens. But this is not true. Animal courtship can be very formal. An animal that is ready to mate sends out a signal saying, "I am ready to mate." Members of the opposite sex read the signal and, if they also are ready, respond by showing interest. This frigatebird, for example, is signaling readiness with its red throat pouch. The pouch forms at the time of year when he is almost ready to breed. When he is ready, he blows it up like a balloon, throwing back his head, and spreading and shaking his black wings. Female frigatebirds that fly overhead see this display. If they too are ready to breed, they circle and land close by.

It does not always work immediately, it could take time. He may attract other females, while a female investigates other males. Eventually they settle, exchange more signals and get used to having each other around. Mating, nest-building, laying, and incubation of eggs follows. Other animals advertise for partners in similar ways.

Singing and leaping

Courting whales do not have brilliant colors, but advertise in other ways. Some sing long songs that travel hundreds of miles through the oceans. When groups of humpback whales meet, males leap repeatedly out of the water – possibly to attract partners.

Antlers

Antlers grow each spring from the skulls of male deer and are shed by early winter. Males grow larger antlers each year. Big antlers signal a mature, healthy buck – attractive to females and a warning to rival males.

Wing song

Crickets, similar to grasshoppers, chirrup musically throughout long summer evenings. There are hundreds of species, each with a distinctive song, which males use to attract females. The sound comes not from the throat, but from rubbing the edges of the wings together.

A splendid tail

Peafowl live wild in the jungles of Africa, India, and the Far East. The blue-green ones most often domesticated originated in India and Sri Lanka. Peahens are comparatively dull, with no tails to speak of. Peacocks have the magnificent, many-feathered tails that they spread like a fan and shake when a peahen comes by.

Holding the Attraction

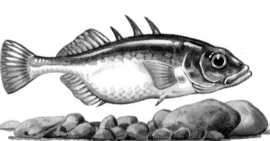

Shining a light

Not really worms, glowworms are wingless female beetles that, within the last three segments of their body, produce an eerie yellow light. Climbing onto leaves on warm summer evenings, glowworms shine their light as an attraction to flying males. Males also carry a light, but a much smaller one.

Signaling (pages 32-33) attracts a mate, but what happens next? Male bowerbirds have one answer: They dazzle potential partners with a show of art. A bower is a patch of ground in which the male arranges grasses and leaves, decorated with berries and other bright objects. Bowerbirds that live in towns often incorporate coins, colored plastic, glass, and other man-made objects that they find appealing.

This blue satin bowerbird of eastern Australia favors blue objects. He will attract a succession of hens to his bower, holding their attention by dancing and playing with the decorations, which they inspect with interest. If they are ready, he mates with them. Then the hens go off on their own to nest, lay eggs, and raise their families.

The bower is a kind of decorated nest, which holds the hens' interest. Other animals have similar, though often simpler, ways of maintaining attraction between partners.

Love songs

Male and female mosquitoes recognize each other, and their readiness to mate, by the whining tone of their wing beats. In very young mosquitoes, the wings beat too slow for their sound to attract a partner. As they mature, males' wings beat faster than females', with a higher-pitched tone. Both sexes are able to tell the difference.

Ready to mate

Monkeys and apes are usually dull-colored, with gray, brown, or black fur and little in the way of decoration. So it is easy for females to advertise with bright colors when they are in heat. This female baboon of eastern Africa has developed a bright pink rear end, a weeklong signal to males that she is ready to mate.

Underwater nest

A male three-spined stickleback (a small freshwater fish) has made a nest from pebbles and fragments of water-weed and has led a pregnant female to lay her eggs in it. Her swollen abdomen was the signal that attracted him. He would not have bothered with a slim female.

Right: A male satin bowerbird has cut down the grass and collected bright blue objects, including a toothbrush, to hold his hen's attention.

Fighting Rivals

Left: Territorial fights between rival coots often look serious, but usually end in splashing, with little or no damage on either side.

Is this a real fight (opposite page), or just for show? Animals rarely fight seriously with others of their own species. If they wound each other, both become losers. It is much better to settle differences by displays or mock fights. European coots – black water birds – flock together during winter but pair off in territories in early spring. Neighbors quarrel over boundaries, and new birds try to force their way in, so coots have every excuse for fighting each other. Yet most of their fights are simply displays. Two rivals face each other on the water with wings raised and open bills. Rushing fiercely together as if about to kill, they stop short and instead splash each other with wings and feet flailing. Who wins or loses? It doesn't seem to matter. All find room and breed happily in the end. It's the same with donkeys, camels, and moose. But some animals, such as dragonflies, fight for real.

Pricking ears
Donkeys have sharp teeth and hard hoofs, and they can hurt each other badly. Yet in herds they seldom fight. Older ones, when agitated, prick their ears and show their teeth. Younger ones show submission with flat ears and a lowered head.

Necking
A camel's main weapons are its teeth, which can cut and tear in a serious fight. Fighting males "neck" – wrap their necks together so neither can bite, and push hard instead.

Handy antlers
The fearsome-looking, 6-foot-wide antlers of a big moose are too big and heavy for slashing. Moose use them as a shield and forklift. A moose can pick up a wolf and throw it over his shoulder. Rival males lock antlers and push against each other. But big antlers are probably most useful for the message they carry: "I'm a big male, so don't mess with me."

Dragons attacking
Dozens of species of dragonflies – lively insects with long slender body and narrow paired wings – buzz like tiny helicopters over ponds and streams. The biggest are more than 5 inches (13 cm) long, with wings spanning 6 inches (15 cm) or more. The name reflects their habits as fierce predators of other insects. Male dragonflies take up territories, perhaps a length of stream bank or reed bed, which they patrol. There they catch and eat other insects in flight, mate with passing females, and fight furiously with other males of their own species that try to intrude.

Honeybees that find a rich source
of pollen or nectar tell other bees
in the hive precisely where to find
it by dancing.

Show the Way

Long-distance flights

How do these migrating geese find their way to the Arctic each year? Scientists say they can navigate by the sun and stars, but experience

comes into it too. Often the leaders are older birds that have made the journey many times before. They would have learned from an earlier generation of older birds – and so on back in time.

So bees buzz to tell each other what is going on? Not really; buzzing is just the noise their wings make. They tell each other important things by "dancing." Worker bees spend all their time hunting for their main foods, pollen and nectar. When one bee finds a good source of food, it flies back to the hive and tells other bees about it in a dance it performs on the vertical surface of a honeycomb. It runs a few steps up and down, turning left or right and returning in a figure eight, all the time wiggling its tail. Then it does it again and again. Groups of other bees watch closely. The angle that the dancer turns to left or right tells them the direction – how much to the left or right of the sun they will have to fly. The amount of tail-wiggling tells them how far they need to go. Following these directions will save them a lot of time and effort.

Leaving a trail

Wood ants live in huge colonies in and underneath heaps of woodland debris. From these, worker ants go out every day to find food. How do they find their way back? Each ant leaves a thin, narrow scent trail that it and others from the same colony can recognize and follow home.

Trackers

Though we make major use of sight and hearing, dogs use their nose to pick up scents. Living close to the ground, this bloodhound sees very little and probably hears less. But its keen sense of smell picks up tiny scent traces and tracks them for miles across country.

Well-trodden routes

Birds fly, but mammals, like elephants, have to walk. Elephants of the African plains travel miles each year in search of water and good forage. Again, the older animals with many years' experience lead the way. Information passes wordlessly to the younger ones trotting behind, who learn the paths and routes as they go.

Friend or Foe?

Books tell us that parents and offspring recognize each other instinctively. Maybe, but how? How does a newborn know which of the animals around it are parents, friends, or enemies? Mammals and birds depend heavily on parents for the first weeks or months of life. Parents and offspring need to recognize each other right from the start.

Recognition is especially important for fur seals, whose pups are born in crowded colonies, with adults fighting and mating all around them for the first month and more. Born head-first, the pup starts calling and the mother replying even before it leaves the birth canal. These are special, individual calls that both will recognize in the weeks ahead. During the first few hours they learn to recognize each other's special smells. So, even if the pup is with a dozen more that look exactly like it, mother and pup will find each other first by call, then by scent.

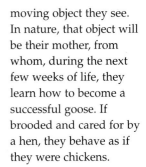

Relying on sight
Many animals rely on scent or sound for identification, but geese rely on sight. Goslings leaving the nest immediately on hatching follow the first large moving object they see. In nature, that object will be their mother, from whom, during the next few weeks of life, they learn how to become a successful goose. If brooded and cared for by a hen, they behave as if they were chickens.

Friend or foe?
We recognize each other by sight rather than scent. To honeybees, scent is all-important. At the entrance to every hive stand several sentinel bees checking the scent of returning workers. Those that carry the smell of the hive are allowed to pass. Those that don't are attacked and killed.

Calling and bawling
Sheep in a flock have a problem similar to fur seals – recognizing their young among the crowd. Again, both sound and scent are important. Ewes call constantly to their lambs, lambs bawl constantly in reply, and both sniff each other continuously.

Left: Fur seals breeding in large, busy colonies have difficulty keeping track of their pups. Mothers and pups recognize each other by sound and scent.

Homing in
In a large colony of king penguins, thousands of identical-looking adults are parents of thousands of identical-looking chicks. How does a parent find its own chick? It stands at the edge of the colony, giving the call that the chick first heard when it was still in the egg. The chick replies with its own individual call, and the two home in on each other.

Learn by Play

Going fishing

A young brown bear has lots to learn. Instead of school, it stays with its mother for more than a year, watching and learning new tricks every day. Today it is catching salmon. The cub watches, then tries for itself. The fish are slippery, the water is cold and wet, but the cub's first salmon tastes pretty good.

Life in the animal kingdom is serious, and there's no time for play. Not true: Lots of animals play, especially young mammals, who have a lot to learn in life. They race, roll, fight, climb, throw, and chase – all things they will do for real when they grow up. Playing together is important communication, through which young animals learn much from each other. These two half-grown European badger cubs, waiting for their parents to bring food, are play-fighting – rolling together with jaws gaping, teeth snapping, and claws spread, to a soundtrack of grunts, growls, and squeals. Their teeth are sharp and the muscles strong. But they are signaling "play" to each other. If this were real, there would be torn flesh and blood. It is practice, developing tricks and skills that will be useful to them later in life. In a few weeks, they may be fighting real rivals for territory, a mate, or a share of scarce food.

Cat and mouse game

Kittens also have skills to learn from their mothers. This cat has caught a mouse and brought it back to the nest. The mouse, half stunned, cannot run away, so the kittens have chances to catch it over and over again. A cruel business? Perhaps, but that's nature.

Digging for food

Digging a hole in a termite's nest with your toes and fingers takes skill as well as energy. That is how pangolins of Africa and Asia make their living. Young pangolins start by watching Mother, then dig alongside her for a tasty reward of termites.

Opposite page: Badger cubs play-fight during their long hours of waiting for their parents to return with food.

Taking your share

Dogs, foxes, and wolves often have to tear meat, either from a dead animal, or splitting a large piece between them. Domestic puppies practice this skill when playing tug-of-war with a blanket.

These young jackals are learning the same technique by tugging at a stick. When the time comes to tear meat, they will know exactly what to do.

Watch my Face

Humans use facial expressions a lot. We watch and read each other's faces all the time for clues to what we are thinking. What about apes, our nearest kin, whose faces can be as expressive as our own? Can we tell what they are thinking or feeling? Most animals have deadpan faces. Watch a cockroach, a codfish, or a hermit crab all day, and you'll see no changes of expression. A few birds (such as the cockatoo, bottom right) change their appearance as their moods change. Mammals have the most mobile and expressive faces. Throughout this book you see how lips, eyes, ears, and other features alter as a mammal's mood changes, and how mammals use these different expressions as social signals. What do these four chimpanzee faces tell us? Not always what we would read if they were human. Loose lips, for example, may signal contentment, whereas a tight-lipped grin shows fear or anger rather than amusement. But they are four different expressions that chimpanzees themselves learn to interpret, just as we learn to read the faces of parents and friends.

Grimacing and twittering

Weasels – small mammals that hunt birds and other small mammals – grimace and twitter when they see a likely victim and approach for the kill. Chattering indicates the weasel's excitement, but it also seems to fascinate the victim, perhaps making it easier to catch.

Mood changes

Though less expressive than chimpanzees, baboons have faces that change with their moods. When an old baboon sits on the edge of its troop, watching the behavior of others, you see constant shifts of facial expression – eyebrows twitching, brows wrinkling, eyes widening or closing, ears moving back and forward, lips curling – all signaling rapid shifts of mood. Other baboons recognize and respond to the signals.

Nodding and humming

Elephants show their moods in movements of their probing trunks and flapping ears. At ease within the herd, they nod and hum quietly to each other, swaying gently with eyes half-closed. When troubled or puzzled, they stop humming, stand firm, and stare wide-eyed, with ears forward and alert.

Showing emotions

Cockatoos are parrots with head crests of long feathers that rise and fall with their moods. The sulfur-crested cockatoo on the right, with crest laid back, is at peace with the world. The one on the left, with crest raised, is interested, excited, or angry.

Opposite page: Chimpanzees' feelings are reflected in their facial expressions, from calm (top right), increasingly agitated, to angry (bottom).

Mutual Cooperation

Cleaning and grooming

Sunfish are large round fish up to 6 ft. (nearly 2 m) in diameter that swim slowly through tropical seas. Small parasites of all kinds gather on their skin, feeding on their blood and probably making them feel itchy. They cannot clean themselves, but other fish do the job for them. Here a dozen tiny half-moon fish are nibbling the parasites and loose skin from a sunfish, which stays still to help them in their work.

Animals helping each other? We know of plenty that hunt and eat each other, or steal each other's food or space, but helping one another? Here and there we find friendly relationships between two different kinds of animals from which both seem to benefit. When it happens, it usually depends on good communication between the species. Wood ants that live in nests on the ground (see page 39) forage widely in the forest trees, bringing back insects and other kinds of food to feed workers and young. On trees where aphids – soft-bodied insects that suck plant juices – are present, the ants behave differently. Instead of killing the aphids, they stroke them gently to obtain their sugar-rich excretions, drink the sugary solution, and take it back to the nest in their stomachs. Both gain from the deal – the aphids by being protected and staying alive, the ants by obtaining an easy supply of sugar.

Right: On the leaf of a forest tree, a wood ant strokes aphids with its antennae and feeds on their sugary excretions.

Catcall

Cats like to hunt and kill birds. Some kinds of birds call loudly and attack when they see a cat. Too small to hurt it, they can at least annoy it and warn other birds of its presence. This blackbird's "catcall" has prompted finches and other birds to join in an airborne attack.

Keeping watch

Baboons and Grant's gazelles often appear together on the African plains, cooperating by keeping a joint watch against predators. In flat grassland, gazelles see farther than baboons, but among trees or hills, the baboons see farther. Each species has learned to respond to the other's alarm calls and movements.

Mutual protection

Hermit crabs are strange, twisted crabs that live in discarded whelk shells, scavenging tiny food particles from the sea floor. Sea anemones live on rocks and undersea cliffs, straining particles from the surrounding water. Often we find an anemone attached to a hermit crab's shell. Have they made a deal? We don't know, but the anemone benefits from being moved around by the crab, while the crab gains from being camouflaged and partly hidden by the anemone.

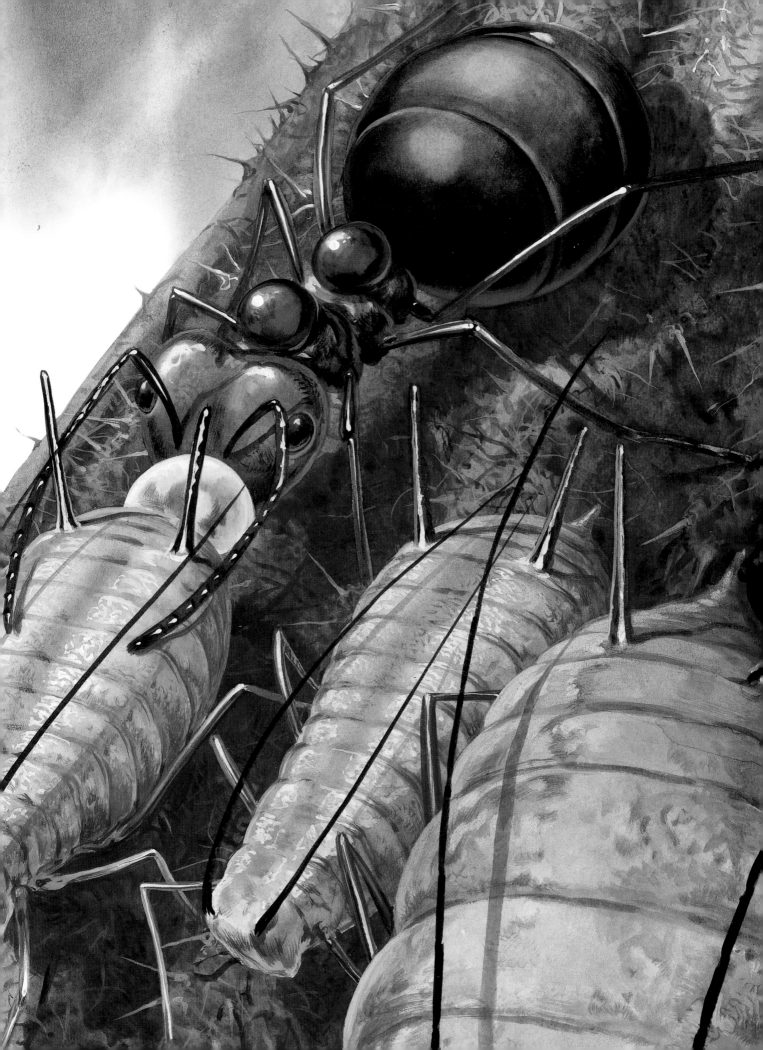

Index

A

advertising 32–3, 34–5
African hunting dogs 30–1
alarm calls 8–9
albatrosses 29
amphibians 21
anole lizard 22–3
antlers 33, 37
ants 39, 46
apes 16, 29, 34, 44–5
aphids 20–1, 46–7

B

baboons 24–5, 34, 45, 46
bad tempers 24–5
badgers 42–3
bat-eared foxes 26–7
bawling 41
bears 42
bees 10, 38–9, 41
birds 6–7, 9, 12–13, 16–17,
   18–19, 22, 26, 28–9, 30, 32–3,
   34–5, 36–7, 41, 45
blackbirds 12, 46
bloodhounds 39
body movements 16
bowerbirds 34–5
breeding season 22, 28–9
brown bears 42
buzzing 10, 39

C

camels 37
caracal 25
cat-call 46
cats 15, 25, 42, 46
chickadees 19
chimpanzees 29
cobras 22
cockatoos 45
cockerel/rooster 6–7, 12
colonies 19, 39, 40–1
color, courtship 22–3, 32–3, 34
color, warning 20–1, 25
cooperation between species
   9, 46–7
coots, European 36–7
coral snake 21
cormorants 26
courtship display 16–17, 22–3,
   34–5
crabs 46
crickets 33

D

dancing 38–9
dogs 8–9, 18–19, 29, 30–1, 39,
   42
donkeys 37
doves 28–9
dragonflies 37

E

ears 15, 24–5, 26–7, 37
elephant seals 29
elephants 25, 39, 45
emotions 24–5
emperor penguins 30
eyes, scary 15

F

facial expressions 16, 24–5,
   44–5
fighting rivals 36–7
finches 19
fire-bellied toads 21
fishes 21, 22, 34, 46
fishing 42
flamingos 16–17
flocks 12, 16–17, 29
food, finding 16, 38–9, 42
foxes 26–7, 42
foxhounds 18–19
friends, recognizing 40–1
frigatebird 32–3
frogs 21
fur seals 40–1

G

gazelles 12, 30, 46
geese 12–13, 39, 41
gentoo penguins 18–19
gifts 26
glowworms 34
gnus 16
gorillas 16
Grant's gazelles 46
grimacing 45
grooming 46

H

half-moon fish 46
head crests 45
hermit crabs 46
hippopotamus 25
hissing 15
honey-bees 38–9, 41
hooded seals 22
hormones 29
horns 12
howler monkey 10–11
humpback whales 33
hunting 18–19

I

iguanas, marine 19
insects 10, 14, 33, 34, 37, 38–9,
   46–7
instinct 30–1

J

jackals 42

K

killer whales 18–19
king penguins 41
kittens 42
kittiwakes 26

L

ladybirds 20–1
lantern bugs 15
leaders/bosses 16, 26–7, 39
leaping 33
lemurs 10
leopard seals 18–19
lights 34
lions 10
living together 9, 10, 12,
   16–17, 18–19, 26
lizards 19, 22–3, 25
llamas 15

M

mammals 8–9, 10–11, 12–13,
   15, 16, 18–19, 25, 26–7, 29,
   30–1, 42–3, 45
mates/mating 16–17, 32–3,
   34–5
meercats 8–9
migration 16, 39
mobbing 19
monkeys 10–11, 24–5, 34
moose 37
mosquitoes 34
mourning doves 28–9

N

necking 37

O

orcas 18–19
ostriches 9
owls 19

P

pangolins 42
parrots 45
partnerships 28–9, 34–5
peafowl 33
penguins 18–19, 30, 41
play, learning by 42–3
play-fights 42–3
poison 20–1
poison-dart frogs 21
porcupine fish 22
prairie dogs 8–9, 16
preening, mutual 28–9
puppies 30–1, 42

R

rabbits 9, 12
rattlesnake 14–15, 21
recognition 16, 29, 40–1
roaring 10, 22
rodents 8–9
rooks 16
rooster/cockerel 6-7, 12

S

satin bowerbird 34–5
scent/smell 10, 12, 15, 16,
   18–19, 21, 29, 39, 40–1

scorpionfish 21
sea anemones 46
sea lion 26
seals 18–19, 22, 29, 40–1
sentries 8–9
shape, changing 22
sheep 41
sight 41
signals, territorial 10–11
singing 12, 33
size, increasing 22, 37
skink, blue-tongued 25
skunks 15
snakes 14–15, 21, 22
sound 8–9, 10–11, 12–13,
   14–15, 16, 19, 22, 25, 30, 33,
   34, 40–1, 46
spitting 15
spraying 15
stickleback 34
stings 21
submission 26–7
sunfish 46
swans 22

T

tail-wagging 10, 29, 38–9
tails 33
terns 30
territory boundaries 10,
   12–13, 22
Thompson's gazelles 12
three-spined stickleback 34
throat pouch 32–3
thrush chicks 30
toads 21
towns 9
trackers 39
trails/routes 39
troops 10
tug-of-war 42
twittering 45

W

wallowing 29
warnings 14–15, 19
warnings, personal 12–13
weasels 45
whales 18–19, 33
whiskers 15, 26
wildebeest 16
wolves 10, 42
wood ants 39, 46–7

Y

yawning 25
young, rearing 30–1, 40–1,
   42–3

Z

zebras 9, 26